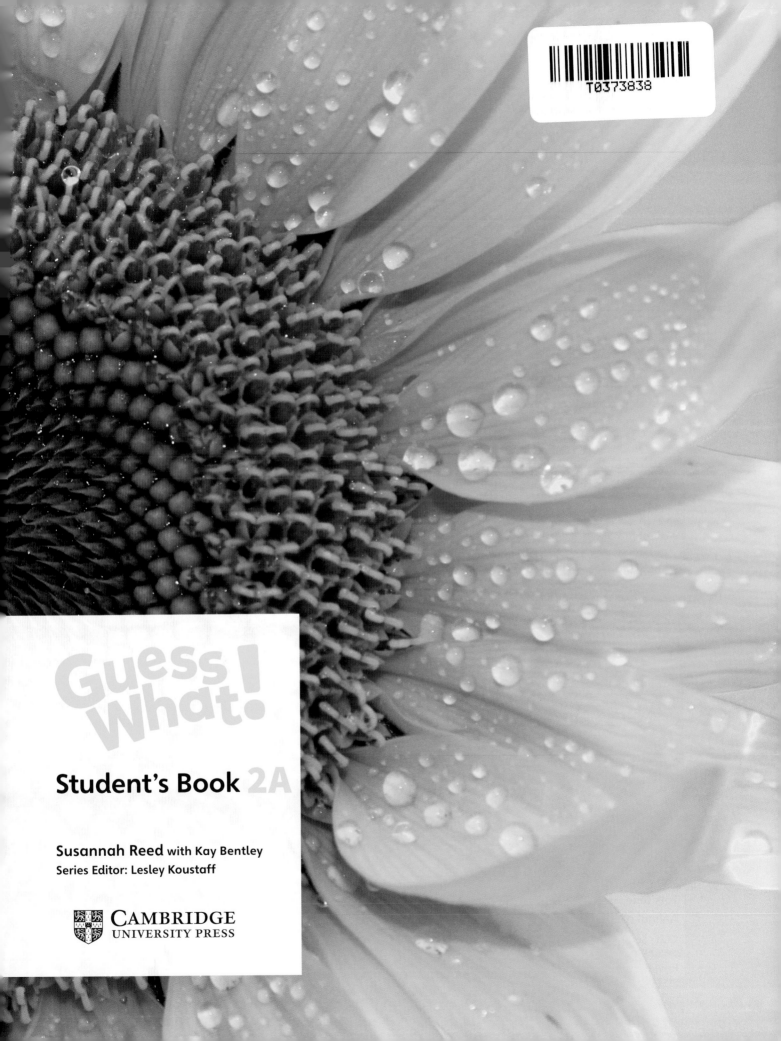

T0373838

Guess What!

Student's Book 2A

Susannah Reed with Kay Bentley
Series Editor: Lesley Koustaff

CAMBRIDGE
UNIVERSITY PRESS

Contents

Hello again!

Guess What!

5

1 (CD1 03) **Listen. Who's speaking?**

2 (CD1 04) **Listen, point, and say.**

1 Ben 2 Olivia 3 David 4 Tina 5 Leo

3 (CD1 05) **Listen and find.**

Find Leo

Say the chant.

This is my sister.
Her name's Olivia.
How old is she?
She's eight.

sister

brother

friend

friend

 Find the mistakes and say.

Number 1. His name's
Ben. He's eight.

Name:
David

Age:
6

Name:
Tina

Age:
7

Name:
Ben

Age:
5

Name:
Olivia

Age:
9

6 (CD1 08) **Sing the song.**

Happy, happy, look and see,
We can sing our ABCs.

7 (CD1 09) **Listen and point.**

Dan   Jill   Sam   Sue   Tom

8 **Ask and answer.**

What's your name?   My name's Harry.

How do you spell "Harry"?   It's H-A-R-R-Y.

9 CD1 11 Listen, look, and say.

1 What's this?

It's a ruler.

2 What are these?

They're books.

10 CD1 12 Listen and point.

1   2   3

a

b

11 Ask and answer.

b, 1. What's this?   It's a red bike.

13   **Listen and act.**

Animal sounds

14 **Listen and say.**

The rabbit can run. The lion is lazy.

What kind of **art** is it?

1 CD1 18 **Listen and say.**

photography   drawing   sculpture   painting

2 **Watch the video.**

3 **Look and say the kind of art.**

Number 1. Sculpture.   Yes.

Guess What!

Project

4 **Make a class sculpture.**

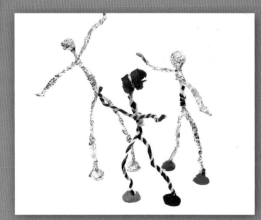

1 Transportation

Guess What!

1 CD1 19 **Listen. Who's speaking?**

2 CD1 20 **Listen, point, and say.**

1 plane

2 helicopter

3 bus

4 car

5 truck

6 motorcycle

7 train

8 boat

9 tractor

Find Leo

3 CD1 21 **Listen and find.**

4 CD1 22 **Say the chant.**

This is my car.
It's a big red car.
This is my car,
And it goes like this.
Vroom! Vroom!

car

bike

train

boat

5 **Match and say.**   Number 1, c. It's a tractor!

 1

 2

 3

 4

 a

 b

 c

 d

6 About Me **Ask and answer.**

Do you like motorcycles?   Yes, I do.

7 CD1 24 **Sing the song.**

I have a 🚚 ,
You have a 🚂 .
He has a 🛴 ,
And she has a ✈️ .

Let's play together.
Let's share our toys.
Let's play together.
All the girls and boys.

I have a 🧸 ,
You have a 🤸 .
He has a 🤖 ,
And she has a ⚽ .

Let's play together …

I have a 🚁 ,
You have a 🪁 .
He has a 🚜 ,
And she has a 🚲 .

Let's play together …

8 CD1 25 **Listen and say the name.** She has a train. May.

Tim

May

Alex

Lucy

9 CD1 27 **Listen, look, and say.**

Does he have a plane?

Yes, he does.

Does she have a plane?

No, she doesn't. She has a car.

10 CD1 28 **Look and match. Then listen and answer.**

Number 1. Does she have a ball? No, she doesn't.

11 **Ask and answer.**

Number 1. Does she have a ball? No, she doesn't.

Listen and act.

Animal sounds

14 Listen and say.

A gorilla on the grass. A hippo in the house.

Where is the transportation?

1 CD1 34 Listen and say.

on land ·   on water   in the air

2 Watch the video.

3 Look and say *on land, on water,* or *in the air.*

Number 1. On land.   Yes.

Guess What!

Project

4 Find transportation on land, on water, and in the air.

on land   On water   in the air

2 Pets

Guess
What!

1 (CD1 35) Listen. Who's speaking?

2 (CD1 36) Listen, point, and say.

1 woman
2 man
3 girl
4 cat
5 mouse
6 fish
7 boy
8 dog
9 baby
10 frog

Pet Show

Find Leo

3 (CD1 37) Listen and find.

26

→ Workbook page 20

4 Say the chant.

mice

fish

One frog, two frogs.
Big and small.
Come on now, let's count them all.
One, two, three.
Three green frogs.

dogs

frogs

5 Look, find, and count. I can see two women.

women

men

babies

children

6 Look at your classroom. Then say. I can see five boys.

7  **Listen, look, and say.**

1

2 ugly

beautiful

3

old

4

young

7 big

5 happy

6

sad

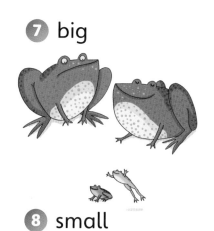

8 small

8 CD1 41 **Listen, find, and say.** They're cats. They're happy.

9 **Make sentences. Say *yes* or *no*.**

Number 1. It's a bird. It's ugly.

No. It's beautiful.

10 CD1 42 Sing the song.

I'm at the pet store.
I'm at the pet store.
Can you guess which
pet is my favorite?

Is it small? No, it isn't.
Is it big? Yes, it is.
Is it beautiful? No, it isn't.
Is it ugly? Yes, it is.
It's big and ugly.
Let me guess, let me
guess. Oh, yes!
It's a fish! It's a fish!

I'm at the pet store.
I'm at the pet store.
Can you guess which
pets are my favorites?

Are they old? No, they aren't.
Are they young? Yes, they are.
Are they sad? No, they aren't.
Are they happy? Yes, they are.
They're young and happy.
Let me guess, let me guess. Oh, yes!
They're dogs! They're dogs!

11 Think Play the game.

Is it happy?   No it isn't.

Is it a dog?   Yes, it is!

Are they beautiful?   No, they aren't.

Are they spiders?   Yes, they are!

1 Look! What's that?

It's a frog!

2 It's Aunt Sue! Hello.

Oh, dear! She's sad.

3 Can we help?

Yes, please. I can't find my cat.

4 Mr. Tom. He's big ... and he's beautiful!

What's his name?

5 What's that?

6 Thank you.

You're welcome!

30   Value: Be helpful

→ Workbook page 24

Listen and act.

Animal sounds

  Listen and say.

A fox with a fish. A vulture with vegetables.

What do animals need?

1 CD1 49 **Listen and say.**

water   food   shelter

2 **Watch the video.**

3 **Look and say *water*, *food*, or *shelter*.**

Number 1. Water.   Yes!

Guess What!

Project

4 **Draw a home for a pet.**

Review Units 1 and 2

1 Look and say the words. Number 1. Bus.

2 (CD1 50) Listen and say the color.

Tony   Anna   May   Bill

3 Play the game.

What's this? / What are these?	How do you spell ... ?	What does he/she have?	Is he / Are they ... ?
1	2	3	4

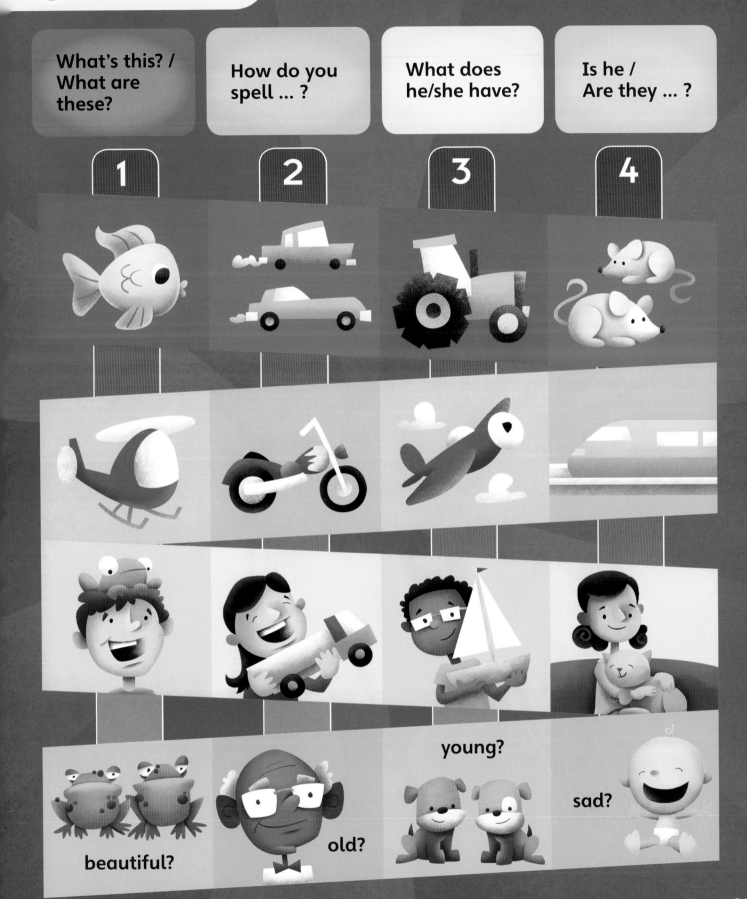

beautiful? old? young? sad?

3 Clothes

Guess
What!

1 CD1 52 Listen. Who's speaking?

2 CD1 53 Listen, point, and say.

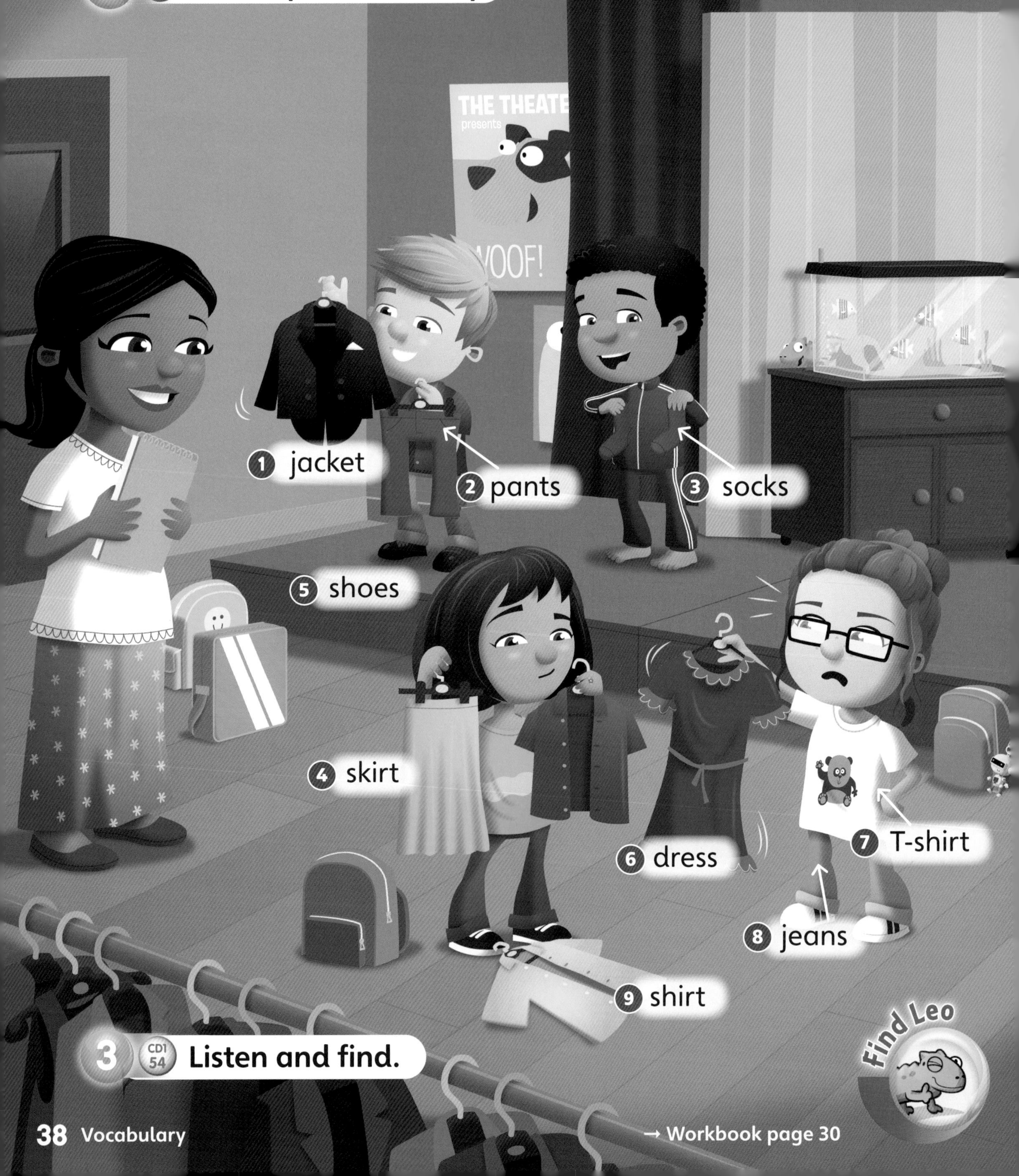

THE THEATER presents
WOOF!
1 jacket
2 pants
3 socks
5 shoes
4 skirt
6 dress
7 T-shirt
8 jeans
9 shirt
Find Leo

3 CD1 54 Listen and find.

→ Workbook page 30

4 CD1 55 Say the chant.

red jacket

green T-shirt

purple shoes

blue pants

Here's your jacket,
Your favorite red jacket.
Put on your jacket,
Let's go out and play.

Here are your shoes,
Your favorite purple shoes.
Put on your shoes,
Let's go out and play.

5 Think Find the mistakes and say.

His T-shirt isn't red. It's yellow.

Her shoes aren't orange. They're red.

6 (CD1 57) **Sing the song.**

What are you wearing?
What are you wearing?
What are you wearing today?

I'm wearing red
And a green .
I'm wearing a blue
And a yellow
Oh! I look great today!

I'm wearing blue
And an orange  .
I'm wearing a green
And a purple
Oh! I look great today!

7 (CD1 58) (Think) **Listen and say the name.**

Sammy   Sally

8 (About Me) **Ask and answer.**

What are you wearing today?   I'm wearing a blue skirt.

9 CD1 59 **Listen, look, and say.**

1 Are you wearing a blue T-shirt?

2 Are you wearing brown shoes?

Yes, I am.

No, I'm not.

10 CD1 60 **Listen and point. Then play the game.**

Pink. Pants.
Are you wearing pink pants?

No, I'm not. My turn!

Grammar: *Are you wearing a blue T-shirt?* **41**

1

Look at these clothes!

Here's a hat for you!

2

What are you wearing?

They're clothes for a party!

3

A party?

Yes, look! I'm wearing big pants and long shoes.

4

Here you are, iPal. You can use my hat.

Thank you.

And my jacket.

5

Look at me!

Fantastic!

6

First prize ... The robot!

Thanks. But I'm not a robot!

42 Value: Share things

→ Workbook page 34

Listen and act.

Animal sounds

13 CD1 65 **Listen and say.**

Jackals don't like **j**ello. **Y**aks don't like **y**ogurt.

What are
clothes
made of?

1 CD1 67 Listen and say.

cotton   silk   leather   wool

2 Watch the video.

3 Look and say the material.

Number 1. Wool.   Yes!

Guess What!

Project

4 Make a collage of clothes from different countries.

4 Rooms

Guess What!

1 (CD2 02) **Listen. Who's speaking?**

2 (CD2 03) **Listen, point, and say.**

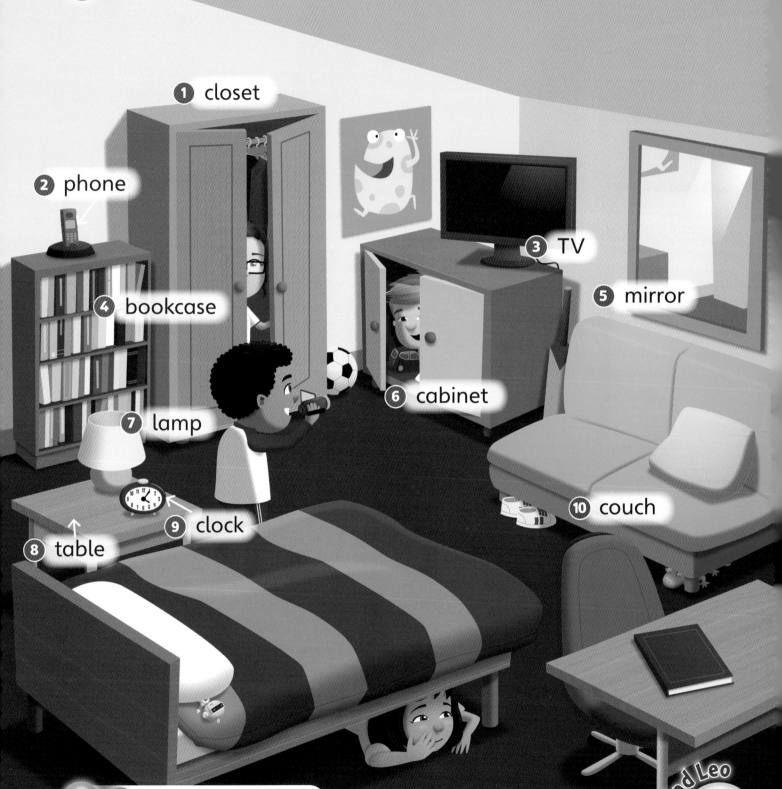

1 closet
2 phone
3 TV
4 bookcase
5 mirror
6 cabinet
7 lamp
8 table
9 clock
10 couch

Find Leo

3 (CD2 04) **Listen and find.**

4 **Say the chant.**

Is the lamp on the table?
Yes, it is. Yes, it is.
The lamp's on the table.

Are the books in the bookcase?
Yes, they are. Yes, they are.
The books are in the bookcase.

lamp

bookcase

clock

closet

5 **Look, ask, and answer.**

Is the phone on the bookcase?

No, it isn't. It's on the table.

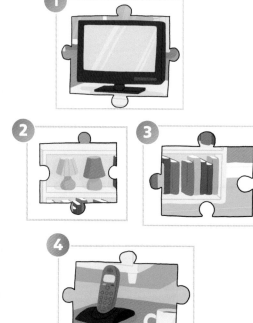

6 **What's in your bedroom? Think and say.**

My computer is on my desk.

Vocabulary **49**

 **Sing the song.**

It's moving day, it's moving day,
And everything's wrong
on moving day.

There's a  in the bathroom.
There's a in the hallway.
There's a in the kitchen.
And I can't find my ball today!

It's moving day ...

There are four s in the yard.
There are two s on my bed.
There are three s on the couch.
And where is baby Fred?

It's moving day ...

 Listen and say *yes* or *no*.

Listen, look, and say.

 Listen, count, and answer the questions.

How many fish are there?

Seventeen!

Play the game.

There are three spiders.   No!

Grammar: *How many books are there?*   **51**

12 Listen and read.

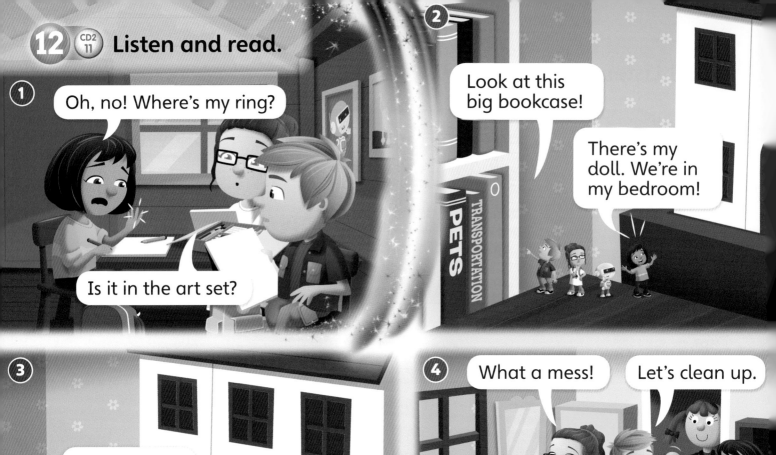

1. Oh, no! Where's my ring? Is it in the art set?

2. Look at this big bookcase! There's my doll. We're in my bedroom!

3. Let's go in. Walk on me! Thanks, iPal.

4. What a mess! Let's clean up.

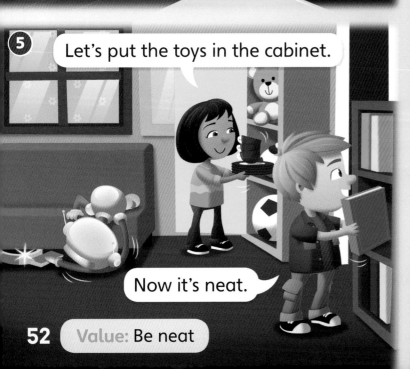

5. Let's put the toys in the cabinet. Now it's neat.

6. What does iPal have? It's your ring, Tina!

52 Value: Be neat

→ Workbook page 42

CD2 13 **Listen and act.**

Animal sounds

14 CD2 14 **Listen and say.**

Meerkats have mouths. Newts have noses.

How **many** are there?

1 CD2 16 Listen and say.

streetlight

bus stop

mailbox

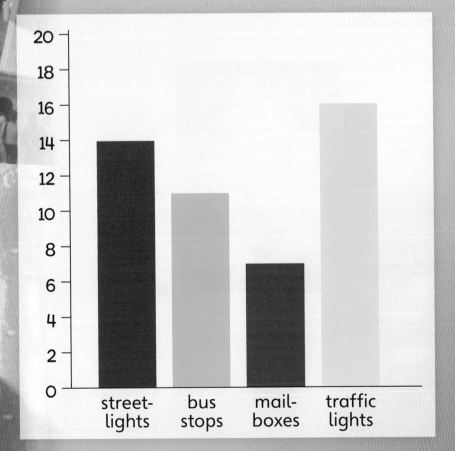
traffic light

2 Watch the video.

3 Look and say the number.

How many streetlights are there?

There are fourteen.

Guess What!

Project

4 Make a bar chart.

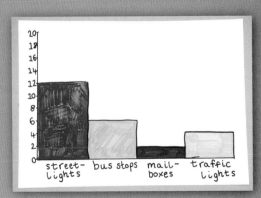

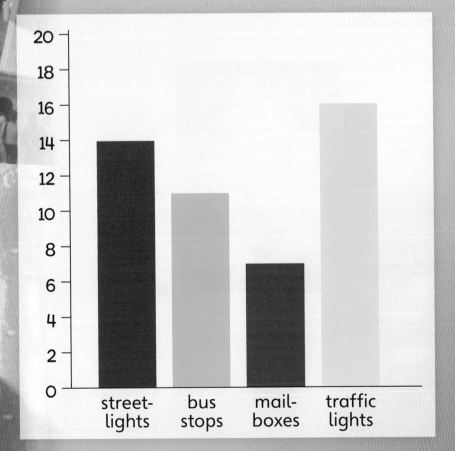

CLIL: Math **55**

Review Units 3 and 4

1 Look and say the words.

Number 1. Jeans.

2 CD2 17 Listen and say the color.

→ Workbook pages 46–47

3 Play the game.

Finish

Are you wearing a ?

17

How many  are there in your house? **18**

Are you wearing a  ? **19**

GO BACK ONE! **20**

MISS A TURN! **16**

How many  are there in your bathroom? **15**

Are you wearing a  ? **14**

How many  are there in your classroom? **13**

Are you wearing a  ? **9**

How many are there in your kitchen? **10**

Are you wearing  ? **11**

GO BACK ONE! **12**

GO FORWARD ONE! **8**

How many  are there in your living room? **7**

Are you wearing  ? **6**

How many  are there in your bedroom? **5**

Are you wearing  ? **1**

How many  are there in your classroom? **2**

Are you wearing a 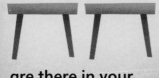 ? **3**

MISS A TURN!

Start

My sounds

rabbit • lion

gorilla • hippo

fox • vulture

jackal • yak

meerkat • newt

Workbook 2A

with Online Resources

Contents

Susan Rivers

Series Editor: Lesley Koustaff

Hello again!

1 Order the letters. Look and draw lines.

1 eLo _Leo_　　**2** dvaiD _____　　**3** neB _____

4 iiaOvl _____　　**5** aTin _____

2 Look at Activity 1 and put a check ✓.

		yes	no
1	This is Ben.	yes ☐	no ✓
2	This is David.	yes ☐	no ☐
3	This is Leo.	yes ☐	no ☐
4	This is Olivia.	yes ☐	no ☐
5	This is Tina.	yes ☐	no ☐

3 CD1 07  **Listen and stick.**

1

2

3

4

5

4 **Look, read, and match.**

1

2

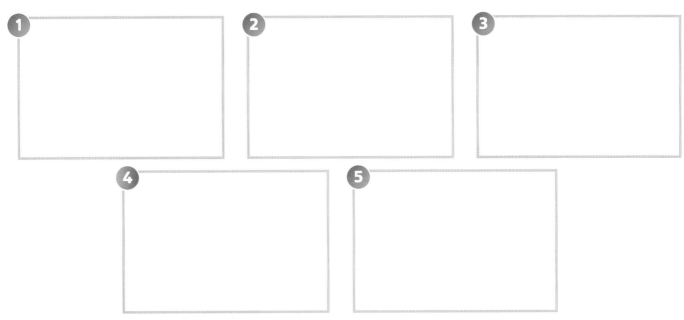

This is my ⟵⟶ nine.
Her friend.
She's name's Sue.

This is my eight.
He's name's Dan.
His brother.

My picture dictionary → Go to page 48: Check the words you know and trace.

Listen and circle the name.

1

(Tom) / Don

2

Pam / Pat

3

Rick / Nick

4

Katy / Mary

  Draw and say. Then write and circle.

This is my friend. His name's Alex. He's nine.

This is _____ .
His/Her name's _____ .
He's/She's _____ .

7 Look, read, and circle the answer.

1

What's this?

(It's a door.) / They're doors.

2

What are these?

It's a pencil. / They're pencils.

3

What's this?

It's an eraser. / They're erasers.

4

What are these?

They're pens. / It's a pen.

8 Look and write.

1

What are _____ these _____ ?

_____ They're books _____ .

2

What's _____ ?

It's _____ .

3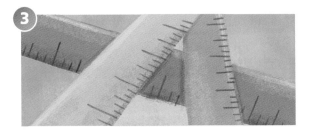

What _____ ?

_____ .

4

What _____ ?

_____ .

a

b

c

d

e

f

10 **What's missing? Look and draw. Then stick.**

I play with my friends.

11 **Trace the letters.**

The rabbit can run.
The lion is lazy.

12 **Listen and circle *l* or *r*.**

1    2    3    4

1 l **r**   2 l r   3 l r   4 l r

What kind of art is it?

1 **Look, read, and circle the word.**

1

photograph / (drawing)

2

photograph / painting

3

sculpture / painting

4

drawing / sculpture

2 **Look and copy the painting.**

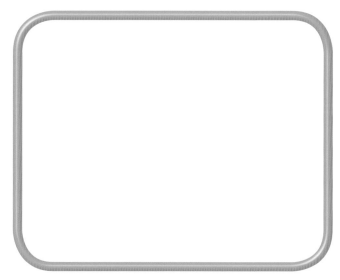

Evaluation

1 **Look and write the name.**

1	2	3	4	5
L _e_ _o_	T _ _ _	B _ _	O _ _ _ _ _	D _ _ _ _

2 **What's your favorite part? Use your stickers.**

story   song   video

3 **Puzzle** **What's different? Circle and write.**
Then go to page 55 and write the letters.

_ _ _ _ _ _ _ _
13   6

1 Look, read, and check ✓ or put an ✗.

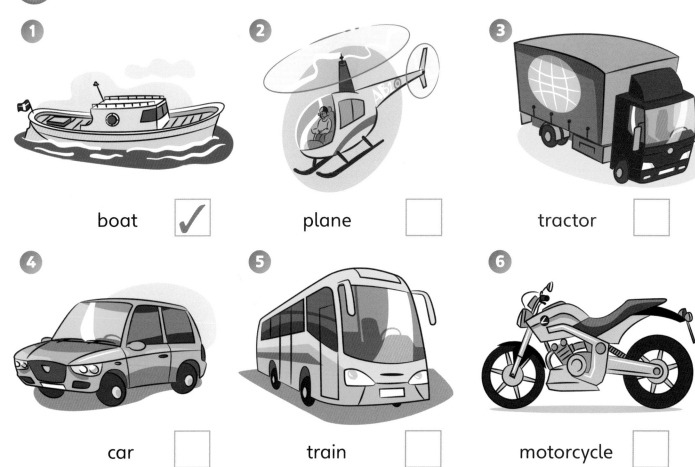

1
boat ✓

2
plane ☐

3
tractor ☐

4
car ☐

5
train ☐

6
motorcycle ☐

2 Follow the transportation words.

Start →	train	truck	ruler	chair
	desk	bus	plane	camera
	book	painting	helicopter	table
	pencil	drawing	tractor	boat

Good job!

3 CD1 23 Listen and stick.

1

2

3

4

5

4 Think Look, read, and write the words.

truck   boat   helicopter   car   motorcycle   plane   train   bus

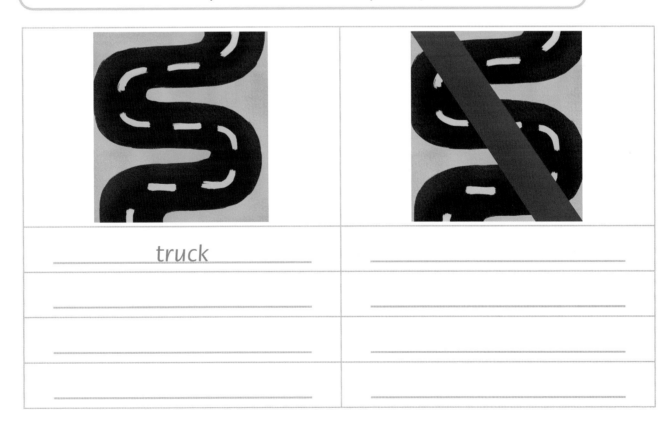

truck

_____

_____

_____

_____

_____

_____

_____

My picture dictionary → Go to page 49: Check the words you know and trace.

5 🎧 CD1 26 Listen and check ✓.

6 Look at the pictures and say.

In picture a, he has a car. In picture b, he has a bus.

7 **Look, read, and circle the answer.**

Does she have a boat?
(Yes, she does.) / No, she doesn't.

Does he have a tractor?
Yes, he does. / No, he doesn't.

Does he have a plane?
Yes, he does. / No, he doesn't.

Does she have a helicopter?
Yes, she does. / No, she doesn't.

8 **Look at the picture and answer the questions.**

1 Does he have a train?
   No, he doesn't.

2 Does she have a boat?
   _____

3 Does she have a tractor?
   _____

4 Does he have a bus?
   _____

9 **Draw and say. Then circle and write.**

This is my friend.
He/She has a
_____ .

10 CD1 30 Read and write the letter. Then listen and check.

a Yes, of course.   **b** It's OK.   **c** Does Ben have a robot?

d Wow! The helicopter is iPal!   **e** Thank you. This is fun!

f Ben has a helicopter!

11 **What's missing? Look and draw. Then stick.**

I take turns.

12 **Trace the letters.**

A gorilla on the grass. A hippo in the house.

13 CD1 33 **Listen and match the pictures with *g* or *h*.**

1   2   3   4

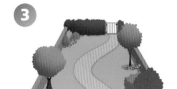 g    h

Where is the transportation?

1 **Look, read, and circle the words.**

1

on land
(on water)
in the air

2

on land
on water
in the air

3

on land
on water
in the air

4

on land
on water
in the air

5

on land
on water
in the air

6

on land
on water
in the air

2 **Look and draw. Say.**

It's a helicopter. It's in the air.

18   CLIL: Science

Evaluation

1 **Think** **Look, match, and write the word.**

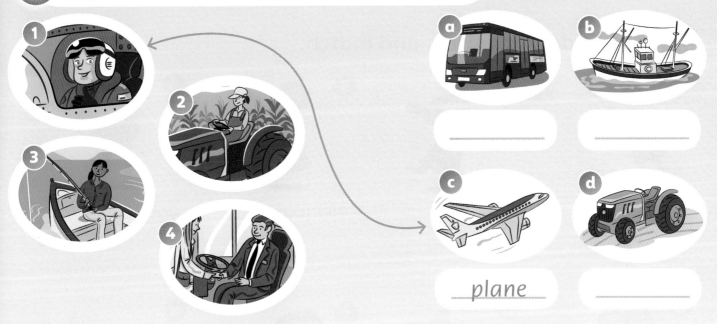

_____ _____

_____ _____

plane _____

2 **What's your favorite part? Use your stickers.**

story   song   video

3 **Puzzle** **What's different? Circle and write.**
Then go to page 55 and write the letters.

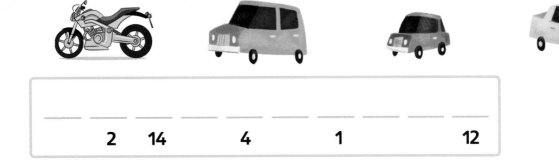

2	14	4	1	12

2 Pets

1 *Think* **Order the letters and match.**

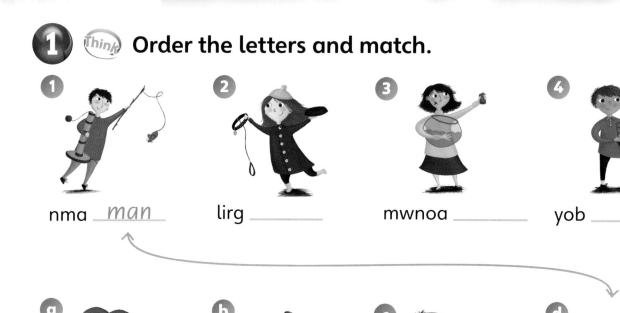

1 nma _man_

2 lirg _____

3 mwnoa _____

4 yob _____

a soeum _____

b hifs _____

c ogd _____

d tac _cat_

2 **What's next? Look and circle the word.**

1 (girl) / boy

2 fish / frog

3 baby / woman

4 cat / dog

3  CD1 39 **Listen and stick.**

1

2

3

4

5

4 **Write the words and find.**

1

men

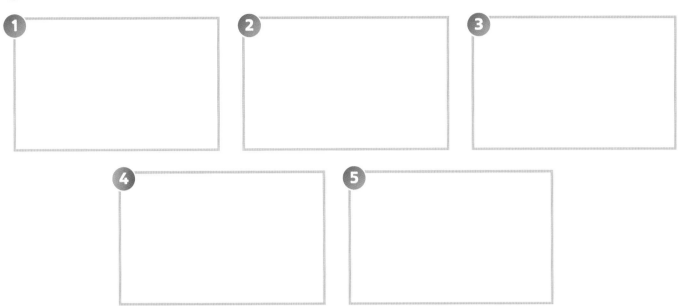

c	h	i	l	d	r	e	n
n	b	j	k	l	o	p	l
b	c	m	e	n	s	a	o
c	y	m	b	c	g	h	j
v	t	m	w	o	m	e	n
m	e	e	t	y	u	k	a
a	w	b	a	b	i	e	s
q	n	e	r	t	f	n	c

2

3

4

My picture dictionary → **Go to page 50: Check the words you know and trace.**

5 Look, write the words, and match.

| ~~ugly~~ happy old beautiful sad young |

1 ugly

2 _____

3 _____

a _____

b _____

c _____

6 Look, read, and check ✓.

1 **2**

3 **4**

1 They're happy. ✓   They're sad. ☐

2 It's big. ☐   It's small. ☐

3 She's young. ☐   She's old. ☐

4 He's beautiful. ☐   He's ugly. ☐

7 (About Me) Draw and say. Then write.

This is my cat. It's small. It's beautiful.

This is my _____ . It's _____ . It's _____ .

8 🎧 CD1 43 **Listen and circle the answer.**

1

Yes, she is. / No, she isn't.

2

Yes, they are. / No, they aren't.

3

Yes, it is. / No, it isn't.

4

Yes, he is. / No, he isn't.

9 **Look at the picture and answer the questions.**

1 Is it beautiful? ___No, it isn't.___ 2 Are they happy? _____

3 Is it ugly? _____ 4 Are they old? _____

5 Are they young? _____ 6 Are they sad? _____

CD1 45 **Look and write the words. Then listen and check.**

cat   ~~frog~~   beautiful   What's   you   sad

1

Look! What's that?

It's a ___frog___ !

2

It's Aunt Sue! Hello.

Oh, dear! She's _____ .

3

Can we help?

Yes, please. I can't find my _____ .

4

Mr. Tom. He's big … and he's _____ !

What's his name?

5

_____ that?

6

Thank _____ .

You're welcome!

11 **What's missing? Look and draw. Then stick.**

a

b

c

I am helpful. ☺

12 **Trace the letters.**

A fox with a fish.
A vulture with
vegetables.

13 (CD1 48) **Listen and check ✓ v or f.**

1	v ☐	f ✓	2	v ☐	f ☐
3	v ☐	f ☐	4	v ☐	f ☐

What do animals need?

1 **Look, read, and match.**

1 Animals need food.

2 Animals need water.

3 Animals need shelter.

4 Animals need sleep.

2 **Look at the picture and check ✔ the box.**

1 A mouse needs shelter.	☐
2 A mouse needs food.	☐
3 A mouse needs water.	☐

Evaluation

1 **Read and write the answer.**

1 This pet can climb trees. It likes mice and fish. _____cat_____

2 This pet swims in water. It doesn't have legs. _____

3 This pet is very small. It has four short legs and
   a long tail. _____

4 This pet likes the water. It has long legs and can jump. _____

5 This pet has four legs and a tail. It isn't a cat. _____

2 **What's your favorite part? Use your stickers.**

story   song   video

3 **Puzzle** **What's different? Circle and write.**
Then go to page 55 and write the letters.

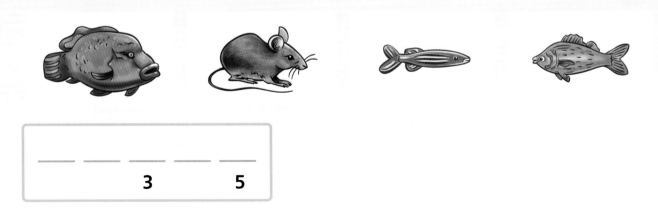

___ ___ ___ ___
      3   5

Review Units 1 and 2

1 Look and write the word.

2 Read and circle the answer.

1 What are … ? They're books.
  a this   b (these)

2 He … a motorcycle.
  a has   b does

3 … babies.
  a It's   b They're

4 How do you … "Leo"? L-E-O.
  a spell   b name

5 … she … a boat?
  a Does, have   b Have, does

6 Is … beautiful? Yes, … is.
  a it, it   b they, they

3 Look, read, and match.

1

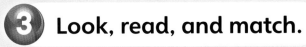

How do you spell "Lucy"?

2

What are these?

3

Does she have a fish?

4

Are they old?

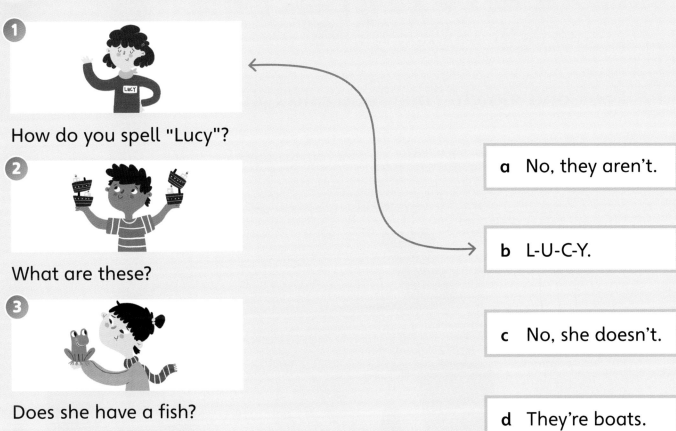

a No, they aren't.

b L-U-C-Y.

c No, she doesn't.

d They're boats.

4 CD1 51 Listen and check ✓.

1

2

3 Clothes

1 **Look and match. Then read and color.**

shoes   jacket   dress   T-shirt

skirt   socks   jeans   shirt   pants

1 Color the shoes black.
3 Color the jacket yellow.
5 Color the jeans blue.
7 Color the shirt red.
9 Color the dress pink.

2 Color the pants green.
4 Color the T-shirt purple.
6 Color the skirt orange.
8 Color the socks blue.

2 🔘CD1 56  Listen and stick.

1
2
3

4
5

3 (Think) Look and write the words.

| ~~socks~~ | jeans | T-shirt | skirt |
| pants | shirt | shoes | jacket |

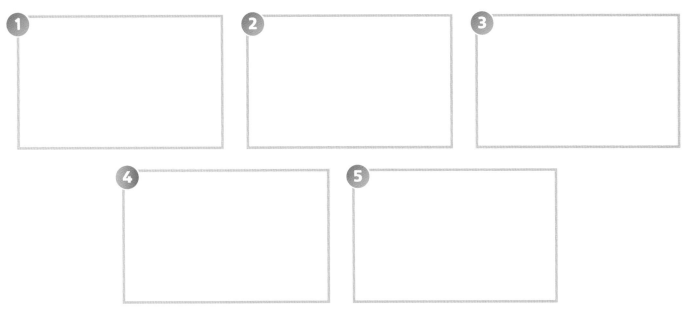

1 _____
2 _____
3 _____

4 _____
5 _____
6 _____

7 _socks_ _____
8 _____

My picture dictionary → Go to page 51: Check the words you know and trace.

Look, read, and check ✓.

1
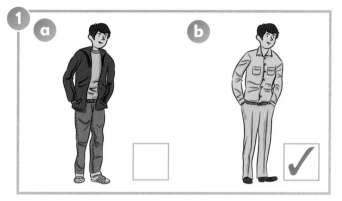

What are you wearing? I'm wearing pants and a shirt.

2

What are you wearing? I'm wearing a dress and shoes.

3
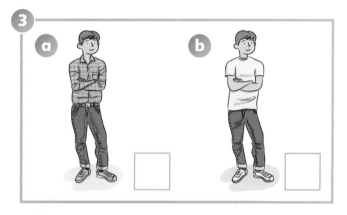

What are you wearing? I'm wearing jeans and a T-shirt.

4

What are you wearing? I'm wearing a skirt and a shirt.

5 **Look at the pictures and write.**

1  **2**  **3**  **4**

1 I'm wearing ___*a skirt*___ , ___*a T-shirt*___ , and ___*shoes*___ .

2 I'm wearing _____ , _____ , and _____ .

3 I'm wearing _____ , _____ , and _____ .

4 I'm wearing _____ , _____ , and _____ .

6 🎵 **Listen and number the pictures.**

 a
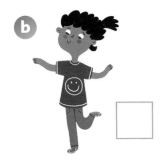 b
 c

7 **Look, read, and circle the word.**

1

Are you wearing a (skirt) / **dress**?
No, I'm not.

2

Are you wearing a **shirt** / **T-shirt**?
Yes, I am.

3

Are you wearing **shoes** / **socks**?
No, I'm not.

4

Are you wearing **pants** / **jeans**?
Yes, I am.

8 (About Me) **Draw. Ask and answer with a friend.**

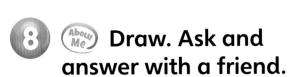

Are you wearing a skirt?

No, I'm not.

Grammar **33**

CD1 63 **Read and number. Then listen and check.**

a

b

c

d

e

f

10 **Look, read, and stick.**

a

b

I share things.

11 **Trace the letters.**

Jackals don't like
jello. Yaks don't
like yogurt.

12 CD1 66 **Listen and circle _j_ or _y_.**

1

2

3

4

(j) y   j y   j y   j y

What are **clothes** made of?

1 **Look and write the number.**

wool [ ]   silk [ ]   leather [ ]   cotton [1]

2 **Look, read, and circle the word.**

wool /(silk)   leather / cotton   wool / silk   cotton / leather

Evaluation

1 **Write the words and find.**

1

socks

2

_____

3

_____

4

_____

5

_____

```
g  s  k  i  r  t  f  s  h  o  e  s  d
f  s  d  r  e  s  s  d  v  b  c  m  q
j  e  a  n  s  n  a  j  k  o  a  l  o
a  w  t  q  o  p  a  n  t  s  p  l  l
s  o  c  k  s  m  c  n  v  b  w  i  k
```

6

_____

2 **What's your favorite part? Use your stickers.**

 story

 song

 video

3 **Puzzle** **What's different? Circle and write.**
Then go to page 55 and write the letters.

__	__	__	__	__
	8		11	

4 Rooms

1 Look, read, and circle the word.

closet / (bookcase)

lamp / mirror

TV / phone

couch / cabinet

clock / TV

bookcase / table

2 Look, read, and write.

It isn't a cabinet. It isn't a bookcase. It's a ___closet___ .

It isn't a mirror. It isn't a lamp. It's a _____ .

It isn't a table. It isn't a bed. It's a _____ .

It isn't a TV. It isn't a lamp. It's a _____ .

3 CD2 06 Listen and stick.

1

2

3

4

5

4 Think Look, match, and write the words.

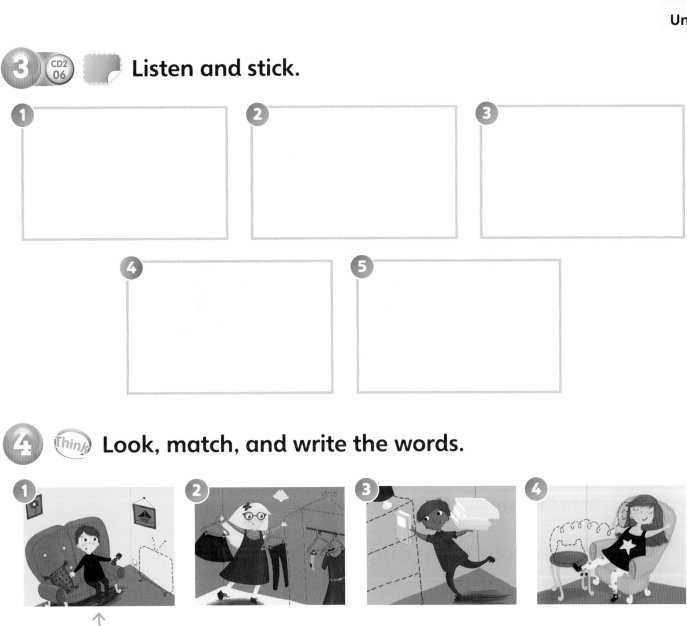

1   2   3   4

a   b   c   d

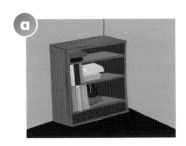

_____   _____   _____   TV _____

My picture dictionary → Go to page 52: Check the words you know and trace.

5 Look, read, and write *yes* or *no*.

1 There are four lamps in the bedroom.	*no*
2 There are two couches in the living room.	___
3 There are two clocks in the bedroom.	___
4 There's a closet in the living room.	___
5 There's a bookcase in the living room.	___
6 There's a mirror in the bedroom.	___

6 (About Me) Draw your room and say. Then write.

There's a lamp in my room.

There are two tables in my room.

There's a _____ in my room.

There are _____

_____ in my room.

7 (Think) **What's next? Read and write.**

fifteen	twenty	~~eleven~~	twelve

1 one, three, five, seven, nine, _____eleven_____

2 two, four, six, eight, ten, _____ , fourteen

3 three, six, nine, twelve, _____ , eighteen

4 five, ten, fifteen, _____

8 **Count and write. Then answer the questions.**

12					

1 How many socks are there?   _There are twelve socks._

2 How many fish are there?   _____

3 How many cars are there?   _____

4 How many shoes are there?   _____

5 How many balls are there?   _____

6 How many books are there?   _____

9 CD2 12 Read and write the letter. Then listen and check.

a Let's clean up.　　**b** Thanks, iPal!　　**c** It's your ring, Tina!

d Look at this big bookcase!　　**e** Oh, no! Where's my ring?

f Now it's neat.

1 _e_

Is it in the art set?

2 There's my doll. We're in my bedroom!

3 Let's go in. Walk on me!

4 What a mess!

5 Let's put the toys in the cabinet.

6 What does iPal have?

10 **Look, read, and stick.**

I'm neat.

11 **Trace the letters.**

Meerkats have mouths. Newts have noses.

12 CD2 15 **Listen and circle the pictures.**

m

n

How many are there?

1 Count and write the number.

1
 +  = ☐

2
 +  = ☐

3
 +  = ☐

4
 +  = ☐

Evaluation

1 Order the letters and write the word.

1 mlpa _lamp_

2 abetl _____

3 ccklo _____

4 hepno _____

5 mrrroi _____

6 houcc _____

2 What's your favorite part? Use your stickers.

story   song   video

3 Puzzle **What's different? Circle and write.**
Then go to page 55 and write the letters.

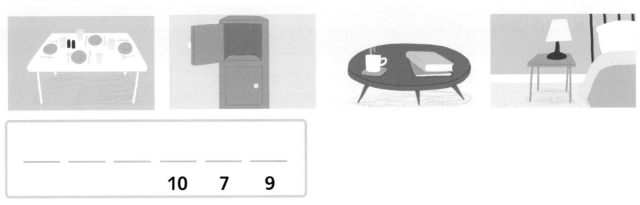

___ ___ ___ ___

10   7   9

Review Units 3 and 4

1 Look and write the word. Then draw Number 8.

Crossword:
- 8
- 1 c l o c k
- 2 _ _ p
- 3 t _ l
- 4 _ _ r _ o _
- 5 _ _ _ e
- 6 _ _ s
- 7 _ a _ _

8 [blank box]

2 Read and circle.

1 **There's** / **There are** a table in the kitchen.
2 What **is** / **are** you wearing?
3 How many bookcases **are** / **is** there?
4 This is a yellow **dress** / **jeans**.

3 Look, read, and write the answers.

1

Is it ugly? _____No, it isn't._____

2

Are you wearing a jacket, Simon?

_____

3

What are you wearing, Grandma?

_____

4

How many socks are there in the closet? _____

4 CD2 18 Listen and check ✔.

1

2

47

Hello again!

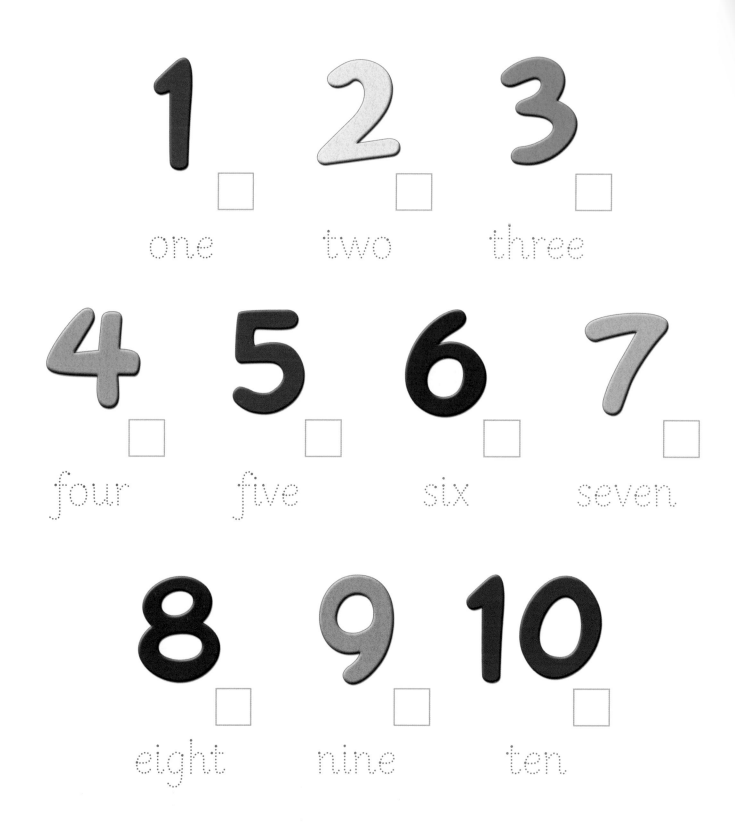

1 one

2 two

3 three

4 four

5 five

6 six

7 seven

8 eight

9 nine

10 ten

① Transportation

 □
bus

 □
boat

 □
car

 □
helicopter

 □
truck

 □
motorcycle

 □
plane

 □
tractor

 □
train

2 Pets

baby

boy

cat

dog

fish

frog

girl

man

mouse

woman

③ Clothes

dress

jacket

jeans

shirt

shoes

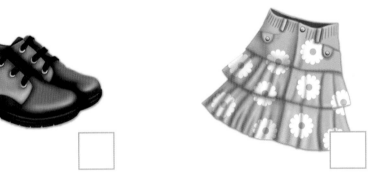

skirt

socks

pants

T-shirt

④ Rooms

bookcase

clock

cabinet

lamp

mirror

phone

couch

table

TV

closet

My puzzle

1 Write the letters in the correct place.

```
_ _ _ _ _ _   G R _ _ _ _ U D _ _ _ _ !
1 2 3 4 5 6    7 8 9 10 11   12 13 14
```

Thanks and Acknowledgements

Many thanks to everyone in the excellent team at Cambridge University Press. In particular we would like to thank Emily Hird, Liane Grainger, and Flavia Lamborghini whose professionalism, enthusiasm, experience, and talent makes them all such a pleasure to work with.

We would also like to give special thanks to Lesley Koustaff for her unfailing support, expert guidance, good humor, and welcome encouragement throughout the project.

The authors and publishers would like to thank the following contributors:
Blooberry Design: concept design, cover design, book design, page makeup
Emma Szlachta, Vicky Bewick: editing
Lisa Hutchins: freelance editing
Ann Thomson: art direction, picture research
Gareth Boden: commissioned photography
Jon Barlow: commissioned photography
Ian Harker: audio recording
Robert Lee, Dib Dib Dub Studios: song and chant composition
Vince Cross: theme tune composition
James Richardson: arrangement of theme tune
John Marshall Media: audio recording and production
Phaebus: video production
hyphen S.A.: publishing management, American English edition

The authors and publishers acknowledge the following sources of copyright material and are grateful for the permissions granted. Although every effort has been made, it has not always been possible to identify the sources of all the material used or to trace all copyright holders.

If any omissions are brought to our notice, we will be happy to include the appropriate acknowledgments on reprinting.

The authors and publishers would like to thank the following illustrators:

Student's Book
Bill Bolton, pp41; Marek Jagucki, pp5, 6, 7, 10, 15, 16, 20, 25, 26, 30, 37, 38, 42, 47, 48, 52; Kirsten Collier (Bright Agency), pp11, 21, 31, 43, 53, 58; Andy Parker, pp39; Phil Garner (Beehive Illustration), pp17, 27; Joelle Dreidemy (Bright Agency), pp27; Woody Fox (Bright Agency), pp8, 18, 29, 40, 50; Richard Watson (Bright Agency), pp28, 41, 51; Chris Jevons (Bright Agency), pp51; Marcus Cutler (Sylvie Poggio), pp35, 57; Gareth Conway, pp49

Workbook
Barbara Bakos (Bright Agency) 5, 6, 14, 15, 21, 22, 29, 33; Gareth Conway (Bright Agency) 7, 15, 20, 23, 30, 33, 38, 45; Humberto Blanco (Sylvie Poggio Agency) 12, 19, 32, 41, 47; Kimberley Barnes (Bright Agency) 6, 14, 20, 22, 23, 31, 32, 39, 40, 43, 47; Lucy Fleming (Bright Agency) 9, 17, 25, 35, 43; Marcus Cutler (Sylvie Poggio Agency) 7, 13, 19, 37, 38, 40, 45; Marek Jagucki 3, 4, 8, 9, 10, 11, 12, 16, 17, 19, 24, 27, 28, 34, 35, 37, 42, 43, 45, 55, stickers; Monkey Feet 48, 49, 50, 51, 52; Phil Garner (Beehive Illustration) 27; Kirsten Collier (Bright Agency) 9, 17, 25, 35, 43

The authors and publishers would like to thank the following for permission to reproduce photographs:

Student's Book
p.2–3: Galyna Andrushko/shutterstock; p.4–5: Images Etc Ltd/Getty Images; p.8 (Dan): Valua Vitaly/Shutterstock; p.8 (Jill): Jacek Chabraszewski/Shutterstock; p.8 (Sam), p.34 (Bill): Monkey Business Images/Shutterstock; p.8 (Sue): Lorelyn Medina/Shutterstock; p.8 (Tom): michaeljung/Shutterstock; p.9 (CL): AnnalA/Shutterstock; p.9 (C): terekhov igor/Shutterstock; p.9 (CR): Wil Tilroe-Otte/Shutterstock; p.9 (BL): Gena73/Shutterstock; p.9 (BC): incamerastock/Alamy; p.9 (BR): Mikhail Olykaynen/Alamy; p.11 (B/G), p.32 (B/G), p.43 (B/G), p.53 (B/G): Tim Jackson/Getty Images; p.12: Robin Weaver/Alamy; p.13 (1): scyther5/Shutterstock; p.13 (2): Chukcha/Shutterstock; p.13 (3): veryan dale/Alamy; p.13 (4): Africa Studio/Shutterstock; p.13 (CL): Serge Vero/Shutterstock; p.13 (CR): Matej Kastelic/Shutterstock; p.13 (BL): Corbis; p.13 (BC): MaKars/Shutterstock; p.14–15: Guido Cozzi/Corbis; p.17 (1), p.17 (c), p.34 (3): Argentieri/Getty Images; p.17 (2): Philip Lange/Shutterstock; p.17 (3): p.17 (b): Margo Harrison/Shutterstock; p.17 (4): p.17 (a): John Orsbun/Shutterstock; p.19 (a): Scott Rothstein/Shutterstock; p.19 (b): V. J. Matthew/Shutterstock; p.19 (c): s oleg/Shutterstock; p.19 (d): Aprilphoto/Shutterstock; p.19 (e): Mikael Damkier/Shutterstock; p.21 (B/G): SZE FEI WONG/Getty Images; p.22–23: imageBROKER/Alamy; p.23 (TL): Buzz Pictures/Alamy; p.23 (TC): David Fowler/Shutterstock; p.23 (TR): Dwight Smith/Shutterstock; p.23 (CL): Bailey-Cooper Photographer/Alamy; p.23 (C): antb/Shutterstock; p.23 (CR): Dhoxax/Shutterstock; p.23 (1): Andrey Pavlov/Shutterstock; p.23 (2): Elena Elisseeva/Shutterstock; p.23 (3): Patrick Foto/Shutterstock; p.23 (4): maxpro/Shutterstock; p.24–25: antos777/Getty Images; p.27 (men): Viorel Sima/Shutterstock; p.27 (women): stockyimages/Shutterstock; p.27 (babies): StockLite/Shutterstock; p.27 (children): Gelpi JM/Shutterstock; p.32–33: SurangaSL/Shutterstock; p.33 (TL): Barna Tanko/Shutterstock; p.33 (TC): g215/Shutterstock; p.33 (TR): Tierfotoagentur/Alamy; p.33 (CL): J Reineke/Shutterstock; p.33 (C): skynetphoto/Shutterstock; p.33 (CR): Galyna Andrushko/Shutterstock; p.33 (1): Don Fink/Shutterstock; p.33 (2): David Sucsy/Getty Images; p.33 (3): BarbarosKARAGULMEZ/Getty Images; p.33 (4): Vitaly Titov & Maria Sidelnikova; p.34 (1): DWD-photo/Alamy; p.34 (2): shane partdridge/Alamy; p.34 (4): Mikael Damkier/Shutterstock; p.34 (5): paul prescott/Shutterstock; p.34 (6): Tsekhmister/Shutterstock; p.34 (7): Olga Bogatyrenko/Shutterstock; p.34 (8): DenisNata/Shutterstock; p.34 (Tony): MANDY GODBEHEAR/Shutterstock; p.34 (Anna): Judy Kennamer/Shutterstock; p.34 (May): Victoria Blackie/Getty Images; p.34 (BL): Willyam Bradberry/Shutterstock; p.34 (BC dog): Matthew Williams-Ellis/Shutterstock; p.34 (BC mice): Geoffrey Lawrence/Shutterstock; p.34 (BR): DreamBig/Shuttrstock; p.36–37: Bartosz Hadyniak/Getty Images; p.39 (TL): Mo Peerbacus/Alamy; p.39 (TR): artproem/Shutterstock; p.39 (CL): Zoonar GmbH/Alamy; p.39 (CR): Irina Rogova/Shutterstock; p.44–45: Tim Gainey/Alamy; p.45 (T-1): THPStock/Shutterstock; p.45 (T-2): Sofiaworld/Shutterstock; p.45 (T-3): smereka/Shutterstock; p.45 (T-4): Randy Rimland/Shutterstock; p.45 (cotton): pixbox77/Shutterstock; p.45 (silk): Tramont_ana/Shutterstock; p.45 (leather): illustrart/Shutterstock; p.45 (wool): trossofoto/Shutterstock; p.45 (B-1): Lucy Liu/Shutterstock; p.45 (B-2): Picsfive/Shutterstock; p.45 (B-3): karkas/Shutterstock; p.45 (B-4): Gulgun Ozaktas/Shutterstock; p.45 (B-5): Loskutnikov/Shutterstock; p.46–47: LeeYiuTung/Getty Images; p.49 (TL): LianeM/Getty Images; p.49 (TR): donatas1205/Shutterstock; p.49 (CL): akud/Shutterstock; p.49 (CR), p.56 (8), p.56 (CL): Image Source/Alamy; p.53 (T): Datacraft – QxQ images/Alamy; p.54–55: Justin Kase zsixz/Alamy; p.55 (1): Radius Images/Alamy; p.55 (2): Taina Sohlman/Shutterstock; p.55 (3): Jack Sullivan/Alamy; p.55 (4): stocker1970/Shutterstock; p.56 (1): Teerasak/Shutterstock; p.56 (2): Kitch Bain/Shutterstock; p.56 (3): Marek Uszynski/Shutterstock; p.56 (4): Pearlimage/Alamy; p.56 (5): Africa Studio/Shutterstock; p.56 (6): Chukcha/Shutterstock; p.56 (7): Nolte Lourens/Shutterstock; p.56 (BL): Bart Broek/Getty Images.

Commissioned photography by Gareth Boden: p.13 (BR), p.23 (BR), p.33 (BR), p.45 (BR), p.55 (BR); Jon Barlow: p.9 (T), p.11 (T), p.19 (T), p.19 (C), p.21 (T), p.28, p.31 (T), p.41 (T), p.43 (T), p.56 (CR), p.56 (BR).

Workbook
p.4 (Unit Header): ©Ariel Skelley/Blend Images/Getty Images; p.10 (Unit Header): ©Robin Weaver / Alamy; p.10 (TL): ©RubAnHidalgo/Getty Images; p.10 (TR): ©Andrey_Kuzmin/Getty Images; p.10 (CL): ©VvoeVale/Getty Images; p.10 (CR): © Pep Roig/Alamy; p.10 (BL): ©iEverest/Getty Images; p.12 (Unit Header): © Atlantide Phototravel/Corbis; p.18 (Unit Header): ©imageBROKER/Alamy; p.18 (TL): ©John White Photos/Getty Images; p.18 (TC): ©Christian Kieffer/Shutterstock; p.18 (TR): ©Matteo Gabrieli/Shutterstock; p.18 (CL): ©Jetta Productions/Getty Images; p.18 (C): ©David Spurdens/Corbis; p.18 (CR): ©Mike_Kiev/Getty Images; p.18 (BL): ©aragami12345s/Getty Images; p.20 (Unit Header): ©antos777/Getty Images; p.26 (Unit Header): ©SurangaSL/Shutterstock; p.26 (TL): ©Evelyn Peyton/iStock/Getty Images Plus/Getty Images; p.26 (TR): ©Digital Vision/Getty Images; p.26 (CL): ©Dieter Hawlan/Shutterstock; p.26 (CR): ©leungchopan/Shutterstock; p.26 (B): ©CreativeNature R.Zwerver; p.30 (Unit Header): ©Bartosz Hadyniak/Getty Images ; p.36 (Unit Header): ©Tim Gainey/Alamy; p.36 (1): ©Robert Harding Picture Library Ltd/ Alamy; p.36 (2): ©f9photos/Shutterstock; p.36 (3): ©Pablo Hidalgo – Fotos593/Shutterstock; p.36 (4): ©venemama/iStock/Getty Images Plus; p.36 (BCL): © Butch Martin/Alamy; p.36 (BL): ©Piyato/Shutterstock; p.36 (BR): ©China/Alamy; p.36 (BCR): ©James Brunker/Alamy; p.38 (Unit Header): ©LeeYiuTung/Getty Images; p.44 (Unit Header): ©Justin Kasezsixz/Alamy; p.44 (L Lampost): ©james steidl/iStock/Getty Images Plus/Getty Images; p.44 (R Lampost): ©Nadezhda Bolotina/Shutterstock; p.44 (C Lamposts): ©nuwatphoto/iStock/Getty Images Plus/Getty Images; p.44 (L Letterbox): ©Nerthuz/iStock/Getty Images Plus/Getty Images; p.44 (R Letterbox): ©C Squared Studios/Photodisc/Getty Images; p.44 (CR bus stop): ©Satoponjp/iStock/Getty Images Plus/Getty Images; p.44 (CL bus stop): ©Zoonar RF/Zoonar/Getty Images Plus/Getty Images; p.44 (L bus stop): ©PÁ©ter Gudella/Hemera/Getty Images Plus/Getty Images; p.44 (R bus stop): ©Anan Kaewkhammul/Shutterstock; p.44 (phone): ©My name is boy/Shutterstock; p.44 (TL clock): ©elnavegante/Shutterstock; p.44(TC clock): ©Dima Sobko/Shutterstock; p.44 (BC clock): ©Anukool Manoton/Shutterstock; p.44 (BCR clock): ©ileela/Shutterstock; p.44 (TR clock): ©PhotoTalk/E+/Getty Images; p.44 (C lamp): ©Antagain/E+/Getty Images; p.44 (L lamp): ©kezza/Shutterstock; p.44 (R lamp): ©Talaj/E+/Getty Images; p.44 (L mirror): ©Petr Novotny/iStock/Getty Images Plus/Getty Images; p.44 (R mirror): ©catnap72/E+/Getty Images; p.44 (L traffic light): ©Rubberball/Mike Kemp/Getty Images; p.44 (CL traffic lights): ©makok/iStock / Getty Images Plus/Getty Images; p.44 (CR trafficc light): ©Jon Boyes/Photographer's Choice RF/Getty Images; p.44 (R traffic light): ©adventtr/iStock/Getty Images Plus/Getty Images.

Our special thanks to the following for their kind help during location photography:

Everyone Active-Parkside Pool Cambridge, Queen Emma primary School

Front Cover photo by Lynne Gilbert/Getty Images